It Is Hot!

By Cameron Macintosh

It is hot.

The sun is up!

Deb gets a big sun hat.

Deb gets a net!

The hot sun is up,
but Pen can sip.

Pen gets a big cup!

Sip, sip, sip!

It is hot.

Dan can go for a dip!

Dan is in a cap.

Jen is hot.

Jen sits at the fan.

It is not hot at the fan!

It is hot.

Tom can go to a tap.

Tip, tip, tip!

It is hot, but Sam can nap.

Dom naps on a big mat.

It is not hot on the mat!

CHECKING FOR MEANING

1. Who has a big sun hat? *(Literal)*

2. What does Pen do when it is hot? *(Literal)*

3. Why does Dan go for a dip? *(Inferential)*

EXTENDING VOCABULARY

sun	Look at the word *sun*. How many sounds are in the word? What are they?
cup	Look at the word *cup*. Which sound is changed when you turn *cup* into *cap*?
dip	Listen to the sounds in this word. What are other words you know that rhyme with *dip*? How many meanings of the word *dip* do you know?

MOVING BEYOND THE TEXT

1. What is your favourite activity when it is hot? What do we call the time of year when it is hot?

2. Why is it important to wear a hat in the sun?

3. What activities can people do when the weather is cold?

4. Would you like to do activities in hot weather or cold weather? Why?

SPEED SOUNDS

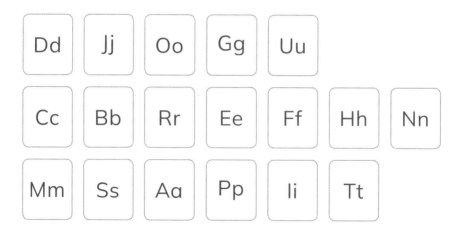

Dd	Jj	Oo	Gg	Uu		
Cc	Bb	Rr	Ee	Ff	Hh	Nn
Mm	Ss	Aa	Pp	Ii	Tt	

PRACTICE WORDS

hot

sun

up

gets

big

Deb

Dom

cup

Dan

but

Tom

dip

Jen

on

not